Fruititude

Growing Spiritual Virtues through Adversity

by Shyreece D. Pompey

DORRANCE
PUBLISHING CO
EST. 1920
PITTSBURGH, PENNSYLVANIA 15238

Dorrance Publishing Co
585 Alpha Drive
Pittsburgh, PA 15238
Visit our website at *www.dorrancebookstore.com*

ISBN: 978-1-6491-3851-4
eISBN: 978-1-6491-3991-7

Fruititude

Growing Spiritual Virtues through Adversity

Sherry's Love

Orangie's Joy

Blupaul's Peace

Grapella's Patience

Strawrene's Patience

Applina's Goodness

Peaches' Faithfulness

Pairence's Gentleness

Waterton's Self-Control

This book is dedicated to those who minister to broken individuals who brave painful odds in hopes of living peaceful and joyful lives full of Christ's love, grace, and mercy. May you and your mentees or family experience abundant life now and forever.

CONTENTS

Frutitude Character Matrix for Vignettes

Personified Character Name	Dramatic Situation	Fruit of the Spirit	Defined	Real Fruit
Sherry	Witnessing a parent's drug use and abuse (addiction)	Love	Sacrificial or Obedience	Cherry
Orangie	Found in dark places (physically and spiritually)	Joy	Great pleasure, happiness	Orange
Blupaul	Cancer strikes a family member	Peace	Quietness, rest	Blueberries
Grapella	Has a habitual rule-breaker for a co-worker	Patience	Suffering without getting angry	Grapes
Strawrene	Despitefully used by a friend	Kindness	Considerate, gracious	Strawberries
Applina	Children caring for other children or disabled adults	Goodness	Beneficial to others	Apple
Peaches	Tolerating bullies	Faithfulness	Constant, steadfast	Peach
Pairence	Moving to new places	Gentleness	Mild-mannered	Pear
Waterton	Experiencing domestic abuse	Self-Control	To control emotions, desires	Watermelon

Part 1

How to Access the Fruit of the Spirit

Experiencing domestic abuse? Working with a rule breaker? Are you despitefully being used by a friend or loved one? Have you ever had to approach a belligerent person in your environment? You or someone you know can answer these questions with narrative cases on the situation faced. Unfortunately, just because you are going through bad situations in your life does not necessarily mean you are suffering for Christ.

Jesus. Watch your "fruit"-itude in your attitude as a primer on being fruitful in your life, even in dire straits, when suffering for Jesus Christ as you move to fulfill His will for your life.

What does it even look like to suffer for Christ? Let's start by saying there are three parts to you: your physical body, your spirit (personality), and your soul. In the journey of life, we all will have trials and tribulations. Always some adversity to overcome.

Regardless of your faith, age, or who you are, if you are human, you will suffer at some point in your life. Our spirit person developed in these difficult circumstances. We are born formable and able to mold into something greater than we can currently see in times of chaos and uncertainty. But there is hope. Hope in what is available to all humanity in the form of a printed text called the Holy Bible.

First, you must decide how quickly you yield to the molding into the image of your creator. In God's Word, we are told of the gospel Truth about Jesus and how He suffered the death of the cross. If we believe in Him, he gives us His Holy Spirit to help us endure adversity. Furthermore, Christ can use your brokenness to further His gospel, which breaks the curse that causes barrenness and sterility in your life. Thus, we would have hope in this life and the next for those who learn to suffer for Christ Jesus. We will need the characteristics of Christ to help us through, which are displayed in the Holy Spirit. You can get through moments of difficulty with the help of the Holy Spirit, which produces fruit in our spirit. In this interactive book, you will find vignettes (brief evocative descriptions, accounts, or episodes), fruit facts, Bible scriptures, and word studies on the nine byproducts of living for God. This is the essence of growing your inner person. You in turn become productive, liberated, holy, have abundant life, and more.

The character vignettes are written to depict the nature of spiritual attributes emerging in moments of chaos. The characters in these mini sagas, or vignettes, are fictional as to allow the reader an opportunity to detach from personal situations that may be real and happening in your own life or in the presence of someone you know. Mini sagas help us to see "Truth," feel "Love," and hear "God speaking" to you and your circumstance.

God is Love. His Love encompasses all the fruit of the Spirit. Enjoy the fruit produced out of your suffering for Christ's sake. This kind of pain leads to eternal rewards and is immeasurable when it comes to yielding fruit that will impact many generations to come. You may know someone, or you may see yourself in the fictional characters named Sherry, Applina, Blupaul, Waterton, Grapella, Strawrene, Peaches, Orangie, and Pairence. Like them, at times, you may think that there is no hope of living a fruitful life here on earth. These mini sagas are extremely short in verse but rich in the characteristics that are displayed when you decide to suffer for Christ Jesus in a variety of circumstances such as

- Experiencing domestic abuse
- Working with a rule breaker
- Being despitefully used by a friend
- Tolerating bullies
- Getting answers when cancer strikes a family member
- Finding yourself in dark places (physically or spiritually)
- Moving to new towns or schools
- Being young while caring for other children or disabled adults

Each predicament filled with pain and suffering is used in the life of a believer to strengthen you. Sin mars the image and production of God's creation. The only remedy is Jesus Christ (John 14:6). Because of Christ and his LOVE for us, we can suffer for Christ Jesus when we learn of His way, His Truth, and do His will forever. It is the only way to restore what God wanted from the very beginning—a fruitful relationship with His creation and a productive relationship with each other. Our lives can be useful while we suffer for Christ's sake. Jesus wants us to be successful in our circumstances.

Using fruit facts as analogies helps us to see God in creation as well as digest his "Truth" in a way that gets us the nourishment at an accelerated pace. There is an urgency to gain spiritual food for the sake of our spiritual lives. We must bear fruit, or we die spiritually and physically. Love requires growth. Jesus even cursed a fig tree for not producing its fruit when He asked for it (Mark 11:12-25). Pray that you manifest what God is asking of you. Bear fruit— one of the primary reasons why you're here on earth. I will say on more than one occasion that we are created to be fruitful for God's glory. It's worth repeating.

Looking at God's creation, in this case, fruit, and how it grows and responds to its environment, is necessary. "For since the creation of the world God's invisible qualities—his eternal power and divine nature—have been seen, being understood from what has been made, so that people are without excuse" (Romans 1:20). God made fruits in a way that you cannot get them without a process, a relationship, and a nourishing environment. "Then God said, 'I give you every seed-bearing plant on the face of the whole earth and every tree that has fruit with seed in it. They will be yours for food'" (Genesis 1:29).

There is only one book that changes the heart condition of humankind. That is the Holy Bible, which, according to its Truth, "All Scripture is God-breathed and is useful for teaching, rebuking, correcting and training in righteousness" (2 Timothy 3:16). This primer refers to the Truth of the Word. The Word of God aids us in being fruitful in our lives, even in our extremities. There are many studies on the fruit of the spirit. Help yourself to any Bible study on all nine of them. This primer conveys each fruit of the soul presented in a case to discover the attribute we ought to have when enduring hardship for the cause of Love. Sacrificial love is emotionless, obedient, continuous, and leads to an eternal place with God Himself. Thus, this primer is not to define the fruit of the spirit for an exhaustive content study but instead to capture what it looks like as it is lived out in the fictional fruit-named characters.

Part 2

How the Fruit of the Spirit
Is Made Manifest During Adversity

Character's Name	Dramatic Situation	Characteristic Depicted	Defined	Real Fruit Associated
Sherry	Witnessing a parent's drug use and abuse (addiction)	Love	Sacrificial or Obedience	Cherries

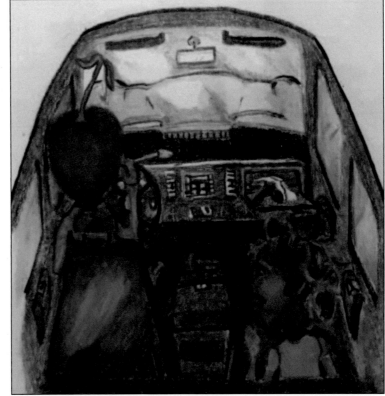

Sherry's Vignette

"I'll take a Dr Pepper and some French fries," Sherry's dad asked the drive-thru clerk while he fidgeted for enough money to pay. After being served, he pulls out of the restaurant's drive-thru in slow motion just before stopping to take illegal drugs. "Sherry, hand me a straw from the glove compartment," her drug-addicted father commanded. Ignorant to her father's addiction, Sherry believes that he is going to take a sip of Dr Pepper once he received the straw. She searches the glove compartment for a straw. Sherry obeys and she hands her dad the straw. The perplexed 13-year-old pondered to herself, "What was the white powder? Wasn't the straw needed for Dr Pepper?" Sherry turned her face from her dad to gaze toward the stars out of the car window. She became discouraged as she wondered, did she do the right thing by handing her dad the straw as he snorted the white powder in his nose while driving off? "Dear Father God...," she began to pray within herself, but it is hard to stay focused while her dad is driving the car now at more than 70 miles per hour in a 55-mph zone, "...please help my father and keep us safe right now. Show me what to do, Lord," Sherry completes her prayer. The song on the car's radio is being turned up by her father, who is now beginning to feel more relaxed and higher. Sherry was not even sure how to love her dad when he was like this. High. Rebellious. Careless. After being serenaded by her father for a while, the time flew by on the car ride. They came to a gentle stop. Sherry was dropped off at her mother's house, which was about a hundred yards away from her favorite place to be...in her Father's house...the church. In the church, Sherry learned how to pray from the preacher using the King James Holy Bible. "Our Father, who art in heaven, hallowed be thy name...."

Recognizing the "Love" Fruititude in Sherry's Attitude

There is nothing right about experiencing or doing drugs. Snorting, inhaling, needle injection, smoking, or any other method of doing drugs is just not right. Please do not try to justify several predicaments in which you'd understand and excuse a person for doing drugs. Wrong is wrong. Covering up a person's drug habit is not ideal. It's not illustrated in the vignette, but Sherry had been told time and time again to "obey your parents." Unfortunately, several upstanding leaders have used "obey your parents" over children to enslave them to a false sense of obedience. The Word says in Exodus 20:12, "Honor your father and your mother, so that you may live long in the land the Lord your God is giving you" (NIV). "Honor thy father and mother" does not mean to obey them when they do wrong, such as using illegal drugs to self-medicate. Ephesians 6:1-3 expands on "Honoring thy mother and father" in that you are obeying them 'IN THE LORD.'

"Children, obey your parents in the Lord, for this is right." 2 "Honor your father and mother"—which is the first commandment with a promise— 3 "so that it may go well with you and that you may enjoy long life on the earth" (NIV). It is not alright to obey or comply with the command, direction, or request of a person of legal authority over you if it goes against the character of who God is. So, who is God? God is love.

Love can easily be misunderstood. Sometimes our emotionally centered kind of love for each other causes us to do wrong to please another human being. But God never meant for us to live with that kind of fear. You may have heard it said that the acronym for FEAR is False - Evidence - Appearing - Real. Doing anything to be physically or emotionally loved by another person, especially when it goes against the character of God, is false evidence appearing real. That sort of love is conditional and will never satisfy. Perfect love casts out fear, grows, and is made complete. Love does not delight in evil. Love always protects and rejoices in with the truth (1 Corinthians 13). Love bears fruit. When you mature in your spirit, you become fruitful in life. Only living for why God created you will satisfy a restless soul.

Learning to love where you are planted is exceptionally challenging. Wherever you are, however, you can thrive. A cherry fruit fact is that sweet cherries are very particular to soil and site. They need plentiful moisture at the roots but loathe waterlogging and need a fertile but well-aerated soil. In short, for sweet cherries to grow, the condition of the land in which they are planted must be right. Sherry had been planted near a church. She learned the Word of God that taught her about her heavenly father at that church. Therefore, she was planted in vibrant and well-aerated spiritual soil, which is the Word of God.

Obedience to God's Spirit calling you to follow His voice saves our soul and provides us with a Holy guide that ministers to us in times of difficulty such as being in the same house or car with a drug user. Jesus promises us, Believers, "If you love me, keep my commandments. And I will pray for the father, and he shall give you another Comforter, that he may abide with you forever" (John 14:15-16; 21).

In our culture today, America has an opioid drug addiction epidemic. Sherry's situation is not uncommon, but how she decides to face her plight is uncommon. She chose to be obedient to love. God is Love. Jesus is God. God demonstrated His love by sending His son to die the death of the cross for us. It is not a question, "Does God love us?" Yes, of course, He does. The question becomes; however, do we love Jesus? If we do, we will obey His commandments. There are just a few. "Love the Lord your God with all your heart and with all your soul and with all your mind" (Matthew 22:37). Just love.

"This is my commandment, that you love one another as I have loved you" (John 15:12).

How do you show love to drug-addicted parents? We know the Word of God says, "Honor your father and your mother so that you may live long in the land the Lord your God is giving you" (Exodus 20:12). That was living by the law. Now, today, we live by the spirit when we live for Christ. Having faith in the work that Jesus has done on the cross allows anyone to be right with God. Forbearing the actions of drug-addicted parents is a sacrificial love. Forbearance is patience, self-control, restraint, and tolerance.

Sherry was obedient to God in her moment while riding in the car with her earthly father. She did what her heavenly father taught her, she prayed. Ultimately, God desires His children to obey His voice. Ephesians 6:1-2 encourages, "Children, obey your parents in the Lord, for this is right." The key phrase is "...in the Lord." When living outside of the will of God, children are encouraged to do the right thing to seek a safe place. Believers have access to God, the Everlasting Father, in many ways. God can be a father to the fatherless and a mother to the motherless. It is beautiful to know that Sherry can be safe in her church home and wherever she may be. She did not approve of her biological father's choices, but she loves God so much that she prayed for Him and found her safe place "in the Lord."

Points to Remember about Love

- Pray for your mother and father

- Listen to the voice of TRUTH

- Obey the Everlasting Father, Jesus

- Grow in love with a church near

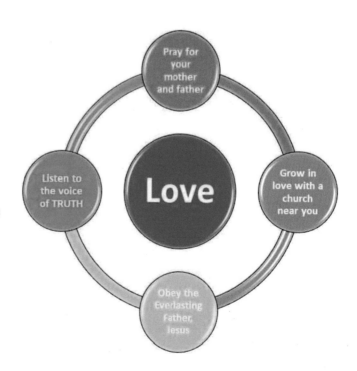

Draw and journal a time in your life when you have experienced sacrificial love through adversity.

Draw Here

Journal here.

_____

_____

_____

_____

_____

_____

_____

_____

_____

Character's Name	Dramatic Situation	Characteristic Depicted	Real Fruit Associated
Orangie	Found in Dark Places (physically or spiritually)	Joy	Orange

Orangie's Vignette

"Living rooms aren't usually this dark," Orangie thought. She stumbled over a few of her classmates sitting in the hallway appearing to be hungover. She is being pressured to do one thing or another that go against her morals as she heads for the front door. She had no idea when she went to the party one sunny afternoon that it would turn dark and dreary by the time she wanted to leave. Fortunately, the first thing you would notice when meeting Orangie is her bright, smiling eyes and a joyous grin. She has a gift of singing her way out of dark places. Her classmates learned to respect her because she is different. Her general appearance is a clean, white blouse with a pair of blue jean

shorts. She blends in but stands out all at once. Orangie knows that this party place is not for her and is not what she thought. Instead of causing a scene and risking a chance of being labeled a square, Orangie sees a karaoke machine and decides to sing. Orangie is a confident teenager because she knows how to use the gift of singing to press her way through dark moments. The song she selected was upbeat, enlightening, and resonated with most of her class. She left on a happy note, leaving the dark place a little lighter with joy in her heart because she knew it was the right thing to do.

Recognizing the "Joy" Fruititude in Orangie's Attitude

Laughter is the best medicine, they say. Laughter indicates that all is well with your soul, and you can laugh at whatever ails you. It seems simple enough. Orangie stumbled to find her way in the dark before she became caught up in a rapture. Rapture is a feeling of intense pleasure or joy. Orangie's heart cried out to her God in the darkness, exactly right where she was. God heard her cry and lit up her soul with a song that was upbeat and harmonious. True Believers of God's Word have learned to sing songs that God recognizes from His written Word. Thus, when praising God with hymns and with the attitude of joy in moments of trials and tribulation, God will move in the darkness. "Consider it pure joy, my brothers and sisters, whenever you face trials of many kinds…" (James 1:2).

Light brings positive energy into harmful situations. The heat from the sun is powerful and can energize greenhouses and other buildings. Similarly, the power given through God's Son, Jesus Christ, is even more potent because He created all things. The Son's authority includes the sun and the light energy it gives off. "For in him all things were created: things in heaven and on earth, visible and invisible, whether thrones or powers or rulers or authorities; all things have been created through him and for him"

(Colossians 1:16). Stumbling in dark places is terrifying. Relying on the joy of God's spirit is the solution to guide you to the light. Take a lesson from two of God's missionaries in the book of Acts. "About midnight Paul and Silas were praying and singing hymns to God, and the other prisoners were listening to them" (Acts 16:25).

When we have sung our way through the darkness of night like Orangie, we surrender to the light of Jesus Christ. You can't hide the light of Christ any more than you can keep a citrus tree under glass all year 'round. They are much happier outdoors in the Summer and enjoy rest in the Fall. The orange fruit needs the sun like we need God's Son. Let the light of Christ shine through your dark moments. Sing out His Word in hymns and psalms. "Rejoice always, pray continually, give thanks in all circumstances; for this is God's will for you in Christ Jesus" (1 Thessalonians 5:16-18).

Points to Remember about Joy

- Rejoice in the Lord always

- Jesus is walking with you even in dark places

- Sing His Word in the form of Psalms and Hymns

- Spend time raptured in His presence

- Experience joy in trials and tribulations

Draw and journal a time in your life when you have experienced joy through adversity.

Draw Here

Journal here.

_____

_____

_____

_____

_____

_____

_____

_____

_____

Character's Name	Dramatic Situation	Characteristic Depicted	Real Fruit Associated
Blupaul	Cancer Strikes a Family Member	Peace	Blueberries

Blupaul's Vignette

The yellow school bus came to a stop near Blupaul's house, as usual. But today is different. Blupaul sees an ambulance in his driveway. In a panic, he presses both hands on the window of the bus. He's shaking in the row where he is sitting. His mother hurriedly escorts Blupaul off the bus so that they can follow the ambulance to the hospital. Upon entering the hospital, they are asked to wait in the waiting room. "This is crazy! Grandma was simply fine…cooking pancakes for breakfast before I left for school." Blupaul's thoughts were running rampant in his mind. "What is cancer? Is everything going to be okay?" Questions swarmed his thoughts while they waited. From the distant hall, a nurse approaches the waiting family and announces, "The doctor can see you now in room 2347B oncology floor. Take Elevator C to the second floor. Your family member's room is on the left." Blupaul's mother walks over to the attending doctor in the room and consults with him near the window. It is snowing outside now. Blupaul turns his tearing eyes toward his grandmother and proceeds to her bedside. The grandmother reaches for Blupaul with her frail arms. Just one hug. Only one look into his grandma's eyes brings him peace. Blupaul smiles.

Recognizing the "Peace" Fruititude in Blupaul's Attitude

There is a unique relationship between peace and chaos when you are a Believer. Peace is the quietness amongst the chaos. The doctor delivers the diagnosis of deadly cancer. At first, chaos from within and without begins to overwhelm the receiver of the news. Then when Jesus speaks "Peace" to the chaotic storm of news and happenings, there is rest, or to be set at one with yourself again. This type of peace transcends all around you. The calming effect is contagious, too. Blupaul just wanted to be near his grandmother in the hospital. Seeing her calm, at peace, brought calm to the whirlwind of questions going through his mind.

We tend to forget that we are all frail and fragile. We are of dust and earth. Jesus did not come to give a sense of peace as we understand in the worldly unity settings. His peaceful order comes in the very midst of trouble. "Peace I leave with you; my peace I give you. I do not give to you as the world gives. Do not let your hearts be troubled and do not be afraid" (John 14:27). Jesus knew that perilous times would overwhelm us here on earth. It is a part of the great Fall of man. Sin, death, disease, turmoil, strenuous labor, etc., would come to every man born of a woman. But God had a divine plan to comfort the Blupauls of the world to know His peace if we believe in Christ Jesus. "He came and preached peace to you who were far away and peace to those who were near. For through him, we both have access to the Father by one Spirit" (Ephesians 2:17-18).

As perplexing as it may seem, it is in chaotic situations that we tend to do the most growing in our spirit and character. Just like acid soil or peat and leaf mold is suitable to cultivate blueberries. It sounds terrible and disgusting to use acid and mildew to grow blueberries, but it works.

Furthermore, partial shade and sunny sites are beneficial to grow blueberries. They are sufficiently hard, almost anywhere. A peaceful believer is also hard enough, practically anywhere. There are bright moments such as Blupaul cooking pancakes with his grandmother.

Then there are chaotic times when a terminal illness such as cancer comes into and threatens the lives of our loved ones. Be at one with yourself again by receiving the peace that only Jesus can give.

Points to Remember about Peace

- Experience quietness in chaos

- Know the difference between Christ's peace and worldly peace

- Do not ever be afraid

- Learn to grow your faith when trouble comes

- Calm is near and far because Jesus is omnipresent

Draw and journal a time in your life when you have experienced peace through adversity.

Draw Here

Journal here.

_____

_____

_____

_____

_____

_____

_____

_____

_____

Character's Name	Dramatic Situation	Characteristic Depicted	Real Fruit Associated
Grapella	Has a Habitual Rule Breaker for a Co-Worker	Patience	Grapes

Grapella's Vignette

With minutes left on the clock, Grapella's coworker decides to punch out early and leave her with a sink full of dirty dishes. Grapella is going to finish cleaning the restaurant's kitchen at the close. Grapella mumbles, "I must have the money. I need this job." She tries to convince herself that busting out is not worth it. She is the oldest sibling in her family of five. Her mother counts on her to work and help pay bills. Doing way more than her fair share, Grapella is feeling the weight of the world on her shoulders. "Suffer now. Reward later." She repeats the chant. Another hour passes as she dreams of graduating from college and becoming a schoolteacher. Grapella glances at the clock as she scrubs down the convection oven in the pizza parlor. Knowing that she has only one more hour to go, she decides to pass the time doing the greasy chore by meditating on a few promises she learned in Sunday school. "They that wait on the Lord shall renew their strength," she contemplates. She decided to praise while she worked. Her heart was lifted. Grapella began to use the remaining time to do some additional deep cleaning. She was able to even remember a few guests she served that made her overall workday memorable. Pretty soon, Grapella's frown turns into a smile.

Recognizing the "Patience" Fruititude in Grapella's Attitude

It crushes ('humbles' is a better word) my inner spirit to know that to achieve anything, I must develop the capacity to tolerate, delay, accept trouble, and plain right out suffer without getting angry or upset. Enduring an inconsistent coworker, a jealous family member, an unfaithful lover, or a bitter boss are just a few relational hinderances for which we practice patience. It is endless to name everything that causes delay or that we would have to tolerate in hopes of reaching dreams and goals. "Of course, you get no credit for being patient if you are beaten for doing wrong. But if you suffer for doing good and endure it patiently, God is pleased with you" (1 Peter 2:20). Also, nine times out of ten, our suffering is going to be for something temporal that lasts for the moment. But if we choose to suffer or have the patience for something eternal and that will last forever, then we, "being strengthened with all power according to his glorious might so that you may have great endurance and patience" (Colossians 1:11).

To work for our subsistence here on earth is the right thing to do, especially if we have committed to a contractual agreement. Use caution against a costly and foolish undertaking or an unwise investment or expenditure. Yet and still, we find ourselves making financial commitments or agreements that are not spiritually sound. If so, we are advised to "...free yourself" (Proverbs 6:5). Ultimately, God wants us free to live a life to do what He created us to do. "For we are his workmanship, created in Christ Jesus for good works, which God prepared beforehand, that we should walk in them" (Ephesians 2:10).

It takes old-fashioned patience to get from a place of working because we have obligations to working as a form of worship. It's a process. Have patience in the Lord to avoid becoming bitter along the 'work' journey. Speaking of painful, most true grapes are too small and pippy or sour to be used as a raw dessert. It is best to extract the liquid content from the fruit and use it as juice or wine or jelly. Thus, the transformation from grapes to wine is a process. So it is when transforming obligated work to worship.

Have patience. Endure the journey.

Points to Remember about Patience

- Develop capacity to tolerate God's process

- Continue in a positive direction on an unpleasant journey

- Work or learn to free yourself from oppressive debt

- Know that you are created for good works

- Transforming grapes to wine pain-staking…endure this.

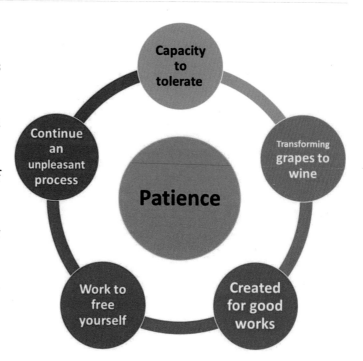

Draw and journal a time in your life when you have experienced patience through adversity.

Draw Here

Journal here.

_____

_____

_____

_____

_____

_____

_____

_____

_____

Character's Name	Dramatic Situation	Characteristic Depicted	Real Fruit Associated
Strawrene	Despitefully Used by a Friend	Kindness	Strawberries

Strawrene's Vignette

Strawrene's kindness is often taken for granted. An acquaintance of hers needed a place to crash after she had an argument with her parents. She was kicked out and had no place to go. "She had the nerve to ask," Strawrene thought, especially all that she had been through with the person she once knew as a homegirl. The former BFF ditched her to hang out with a more charismatic crowd. Strawrene's feelings were hurt to the core because when she loves her friends, she demonstrates it. Strawrene is heartbroken by the ungratefulness of her recent confidant. "She has absolutely no idea how much damage she's done to me." Yet and still, Strawrene gave more of herself to her back-stabbing friend. Impossible, being merciful. "Lord, I don't like what she's done. Please help me love her like you do," Strawrene earnestly prayed. Strawrene, with forgiveness in her heart, asked her parents if her sidekick could spend the weekend with them. Under specific terms, the parents supported Strawrene's decision. Through healing tears, Strawrene moved to show kindness after being hurt. Upon arrival, Strawrene's forgiven friend received a blanket, a cup of soup, fresh towels, and a couch to sleep on.

Recognizing the "Kindness" Fruititude in Strawrene's Attitude

Do you find yourself always giving in an unbalanced relationship? Well, it happens to people sometimes. If there is a relationship, there will still seem to be one giving a whole lot more than the other. The give-and-take concept seems off-balanced to a point where something or someone is going to break. The kindness or grace appears to entirely be taken for granted. All relations are subject to this tyranny, even with the relationship between sinner and Savior. How simple is it to indulge in selfish behaviors while the Savior does all the giving? But as a forgiven Believer, we are not to take advantage of our Savior Jesus Christ and what He's done on the cross for us. "What then? Shall we sin because we are not under the law, but under grace? By no means!" (Romans 6:14).

Yes. Kindness is being considerate, helpful, or gracious. But it is not to be abused. Admit to the Lord when you feel like you have been taken for granted. The Word of God tells us to "Walk honestly in the day…" (Romans 13:13). In other words, let us walk becomingly. Pray earnestly to your Father in heaven about how impossible it seems to be kind to inconsiderate friends or foes. Your character is on trial. Moral excellence reflects God. He knows what we need to produce the fruit of the spirit, kindness.

I relish the fact that strawberries need wealthy soil to grow. Well-rotted manure is used to get a better crop of berries. Spiritually speaking, it is also true that if you get a bunch of manure-like treatment after giving so much of yourself to people, you can still reap an abundant harvest in your life. Jesus can fertilize the heart of the receiver of your gifts when given in the right spirit. Tears of joy flow when you have experienced just how much Jesus has given to us. This firsthand knowledge (which is your witness) allows you to give more through His never-ending supply of Love and kindness. "But when the kindness and love of God, our

Savior appeared, He saved us, not because of righteous things we have done, but because of his mercy" (Titus 3:4-5). I am kind because He was helpful first. Give yourself unto His will first. Then pray, "Please help me love like you do, Jesus." Amen.

Points to Remember about Kindness

- Strive for moral excellence

- Know that God can fertilize hearts

- Always model the kindness of Jesus

- Understand the give-and-take concept

- Know that you are in a sinner-and-savior relationship

- Never cease to pray about the impossible

Draw and journal a time in your life when you have experienced kindness through adversity.

Draw Here

Journal here.

_____

_____

_____

_____

_____

_____

_____

_____

_____

Character's Name	Dramatic Situation	Characteristic Depicted	Real Fruit Associated
Applina	Children caring for other children or disabled adults	Goodness	Apple

Applina's Vignette

"Come change your baby brother, Applina," yelled her belligerent mother. It is late in the evening. Time has run out. Applina places her colored markers, protractor, glue stick, and folders back inside her school backpack. Her homework is done. "It is good," Applina sighs. "Did you finish your homework?" The taut and disembodied voice of her mom causes Applina to respectfully reply quickly and without hesitation. "Yes, Ma'am." Her mother further commands her to get down the stairs and take care of the baby. It seems like a mighty wind pushing Applina, causing her to float downstairs to meet her mother's request. She does not want to upset her mother too much longer. Applina knows

full well what other chores are also expected. This is not new for Applina. Being the oldest of her four siblings, she has learned to work and pray through it all. Systematically, Applina rapidly gives her baby brother a bath, feeds him, brushes his hair, puts on a fresh set of crib sheets, then lays him down to sleep for the night. Applina continues with her regular routine of fixing dinner plates, washing dishes, folding laundry, showering herself, drying her hair, and falling sound asleep with a pair of earplugs to listen to her favorite gospel songs.

Discovering the "Goodness" Fruititude in Applina's Attitude

How do you think Applina shows the characteristic of goodness? Goodness defined is becoming good to help others. That is Love. To grow is a process that builds character, especially a God-like figure. What is the alternative to this kind of trait? If you are not becoming good, then you are giving in to bad choices and habits. You have become increasingly wild and untamed or unwholesome in mannerism.

On the contrary, the act of becoming good requires immediate obedience. In the saga, Applina immediately finished up what she was doing regarding her homework and obeyed her mother's command to do something good, which is to change her baby brother. It is good to help even in times of pressure or dull moments.

A McIntosh apple is a delicious fruit that is a favorite for eating. You can eat it freshly picked, bake it for desserts, or make an apple cider drink from it. Like the many uses of an apple, there are many advantages of a righteous person. When you are an honest person, you also can be beneficial to others, which creates abundant pleasant moments where we all get our needs met. As a believer in Jesus Christ, he tells us not to call Him good. His Father, God, is good. "Why do you call me good?" Jesus answered. "No one is good—except God alone" (Mark 10:18). When we are good, we just have grown in one of the characteristics of our Father...goodness. We cannot be good on our own. We need the help of the Holy Spirit, which is given to us when we have accepted what God's Son has done on the cross. Jesus died, was buried, and rose again on the third day. If we believe this and accept Jesus as our personal Savior by confessing with our mouth that "Jesus is Lord," He will save you and give you Holy Ghost power that assists you to be a righteous person. Just like the McIntosh apple has many good uses, so will we, only in Christ Jesus.

So, in times of pressure to do good, we can. The pressure from authorities and parents may seem unbearable when asked to do the right thing. We can praise a "good" God during our times of difficulty. Be thankful for becoming good. Just like Applina, who decided to do a good thing that her belligerent mom asked of her, even when she was doing something else, that was good. Whew! Oh, my goodness.

Points to Remember about Goodness

- Grow over time

- Help others with all you have available to you

- Suppress bad choices

- Be useful and not a burden

- Obey those in authority

Draw and journal a time in your life when you have experienced goodness through adversity.

Draw Here

Journal here.

_____

_____

_____

_____

_____

_____

_____

_____

_____

Character's Name	Dramatic Situation	Characteristic Depicted	Real Fruit Associated
Peaches	Tolerating Bullies	Faithfulness	Peach

Peaches' Vignette

A perfect ten, was she? Nope. Peaches does not look like a typical model cheerleader. Nevertheless, she tried out for the varsity cheerleading team in high school. Because of the lack of interest in the sport, not many girls tried out. Therefore, many of the girls made the cut and were able to become cheerleaders without much competition. Unfortunately, that did not change the inevitable, dealing with impolite and snobbish teammates. During practice, Peaches knew that there were assessing and critical eyes upon her. Chatty cliques circled in on the latest gossip that they could find, on anyone for that matter, not just on Peaches. Peaches, however, had a solemn request for help for them.

Before every practice, Peaches had the devotion and earnestly spoke to God about her difficulty. Peaches' debonair personality was magnetic for introverted students who in cowardice hid in the shadows long enough to see if she would survive being bullied by her peers. "Peaches, Peaches, big and fat...," taunted her conceited peer cheerleaders. You would think Peaches would quit the team...right? Unaffected by their provoking, Peaches introduced a new step routine that was catchy, trendy, and full of inspiration. The basketball team, struggling through a losing season, began to take notice and refocused their energy on getting ready for the next game. Walking around with a bowed head in constant defeat changed when Peaches put new pep in everyone's step. Peaches was unshakable. Her loyalty triumphed over her weightier issues. To her surprise, the basketball team was not the only one to take notice. "Dance on, Peaches," the crowd cheers.

Recognizing the "Faithfulness" Fruititude in Peaches' Attitude

Time has a way of testing your loyalty to a great cause or causes. For some of us, it does not take much to lose confidence in what we hope. Peaches hoped for an inspired school district. A school district that would rise above the embarrassment of always losing. She even pledged her loyalty to the cheerleading team as a way of doing something positive and proactive for her school community. Ironic that the very support system she needed to cheer her on, which was the cheerleading team, was not there for her. It was the cheerleaders who taunted and teased. Despite their poking at her weight, Peaches was steadfast. She had developed a thick skin to dance skillfully through the blatant harsh words from her teammates. Although it is speaking figuratively of Peaches having 'thick skin,' it merely means she was able to not get emotionally distraught over the name-calling.

The skin of a real peach has color that can range from dull green through yellows and orange to dark red. However, the most distinctive feature of the peach is the soft, downy fluff on the skin. Thick skin, figuratively speaking, is a total contrast to soft, downy fluff on the surface. But imagine still, how Peaches can brush off the cruel words of her peers just as you could brush off the fuzz on the skin of a peach just before you enjoy the delicious, juicy fruit. Just like the fluff on a peach, Peaches shook off the teasing and taunting remarks of the cheerleaders to hold steadfast and do what she signed up for...cheerleading. The district needed encouragement, and she helped to answer the call.

What is it that cheered Peaches on and encouraged her despite the lack of support from her cheerleading squad? Hope and assurance. Hope is found in having faith in Christ Jesus. We know Christ sees the best in us and others because "...while we were yet sinners Christ died" (Romans 5:8). That's how He demonstrated His Love for us. His Love is enduring, so we too can endure all types of unhealthy criticism for His namesake.

Jesus cheers us on by letting us know that, "He that began a good work in us will create it in the day of Jesus Christ" (Philippians 1:6). Go, Peaches! Dance the night away of fear and intimidation. Go, Peaches! Sing a new song of triumph. There is a victory in Jesus now. All the saints of God applaud you.

Points to Remember about Faithfulness

- Brush off despair and setbacks

- Stay inspired throughout your mission

- Hold steadfast to faith in Christ Jesus

- Always live in hope and assurance

- Know that your loyalty will be tested

Draw and journal a time in your life when you have experienced faithfulness through adversity.

Draw Here

Journal here.

_____

_____

_____

_____

_____

_____

_____

_____

_____

Character's Name	Dramatic Situation	Characteristic Depicted	Real Fruit Associated
Pairence	Moving to New Places	Gentleness	Pear

Pairence's Vignette

Banging on his locker in the crowded hallway of students passing to their next class, the new kid screamed, "I hate this school!" Most ignored him. Some of the students just stopped and stared. But here comes Pairence. With a college-prep appearance, he seems odd to be the type to walk up and greet a temperamental newcomer. Pairence steps softly and gently to the new student, then extends his arm for a handshake. Pairence's high-

pitched voice welcomes the newbie, "Hi, my name is Pairence. Sometimes I hate this school, too. Did you know that there is a place here that we can hang out at lunch? Can I show you around then? Is that okay?" A little reluctant at first, the new student pulls his fist off the locker and turns doubtfully towards Pairence. Unbiased, Pairence makes eye contact and prays within those seconds that a fist would land not on his glasses. Thankfully, breathing slower now, the new kid is not as frustrated. He mumbles, "Sure, I'd like to see the place where we can go at lunchtime." The passing bell rings. Just a few seconds now before they both become tardy for their next class. Pairence is happy to enter his class with a new friend.

Recognizing the "Gentleness" Fruititude in Pairence's Attitude

Being frustrated to the point where you will not allow someone near you is detrimental to your wellbeing. It takes someone who genuinely cares about you to overlook your blunders and absurdities and approach you with gentleness. What a friend. Pairence is that kind of friend. He has the quality of being kind, tender, or mild-mannered. "It should be that of your inner self, the unfading beauty of a quiet spirit, which is of great worth in God's sight" (1 Peter 3:4).

What causes a person to be loud? Why the need to create a scene, such as banging on a locker? Dramatic expressions are great for entertainment but terrible for building healthy relationships. When we are immature, underdeveloped, an unconfessed sinner, or just disobedient in Christ, we tend to act out in ways that keep people at a distance. Displaying boisterous behavior at the start of something new is not necessary. Yes. It's challenging to start a new school, yet, you can breathe through a unique experience. Christ himself is always doing a new thing in the life of a Believer. "See, I am doing a new thing! Now it springs up; do you not perceive it? I am making a way in the wilderness and streams in the wasteland" (Isaiah 43:19).

Changing to a new school is good, but if your inner self screams, "I hate this!" how will you see the new thing that God is doing in your life? The pear fruit needs a little corrective cutting away of dead or overgrown branches or stems from increasing fruitfulness and growth. Your inner self needs cutting away of unconscious or wild thoughts that do not allow you to be fruitful or grow. For God to do a new thing in your life, let gentleness take control. Cut away frustration by becoming tender-hearted. Relax your breathing. Avoid becoming frustrated so quickly when change comes. Pairence allowed his unfading beauty of a quiet spirit to flow through his arms long enough to reach out and make a new friend who was not so friendly at first. Isn't that just like God?

Points to Remember about Gentleness

- Guard against frustration and anger

- Cut away negative thoughts and thought patterns

- Know that being gentle in Christ Jesus is an unfading beauty

- Welcome new experiences while being led by the Holy Spirit

- Instead of ill-tempered, be mild-mannered

Draw and journal a time in your life when you have experienced gentleness through adversity.

Draw Here

Journal here.

_____

_____

_____

_____

_____

_____

_____

_____

_____

_____

Character's Name	Dramatic Situation	Characteristic Depicted	Real Fruit Associated
Waterton	Experiencing Domestic Abuse	Self-Control	Watermelon

Waterton's Vignette

"Dad's going to kill mom," Waterton imagined as he watched his mother crawl on the kitchen floor to hide underneath the table. She is battered and bruised to the point where she is becoming weaker at warding off further attacks from her husband. Panic-filled thoughts raced through Waterton's head. "I can't take this anymore. I have had enough of Dad hurting us. Somebody has to stop him." Waterton wanted so bad to become as violent as his father and get into a physical confrontation with him. Instead of just standing there looking helpless, Waterton feels the need to protect his mother, but his dad is bigger. Waterton knows he is meaner, too. "I should jump on his neck and wrestle my dad down to the floor to hit him with something." Waterton continued to drum up plans to make a counterassault on his father. Feeling restless and frustrated, Waterton chooses to close his eyes tight, clench his fists, and pray. He manages to subdue his instinctual

urge to retaliate. Waterton opens his eyes and sees his frightened mother. His intoxicated father stormed out of the house, angry, heading for the nearest bar. Waterton waits for the right moment to speak to his mother. In physical distress, his mother nervously stands to her feet again. Under divine calm, Waterton walks to his mother's side and says, "Mama, let me help."

Recognizing the "Self-Control" Fruititude in Waterton's Attitude

When you are right in the moment of an awkward situation, your first impulse is to react. This is not the best choice. Acting instantly in a difficult situation can cause most matters to grow worse. You must maintain the ability to control your desire to express your emotions in heated moments. Waterton, yielding to more of a calm demeanor, saved himself and his mother from even more suffering than what the moment already had brought them. This kind of calm can only come from the help of the Holy Spirit.

Jesus himself did not react with violence when the Roman soldier captured him in the garden of Gethsemane, but his disciple, Peter, did (read Luke 22:49-51). Even when Peter cut off the soldier's ear, Jesus picked it up and placed it back on his head. What miraculous display of grace and control in the moment of a difficult situation.

Watermelon fruit varies in size. Regardless of your size or age, whether you are big or small, having self-control is likened to eating the very juicy flesh (sweet water) of a watermelon. You see, in difficult situations, regardless of your age, Jesus in you grows more evident as you yield to the sweet communion of the Holy Spirit who gives you everything you need to endure an awkward moment. We all have moments when we want to physically go against something that is bigger than us or that we cannot even see in an inflamed moment. We must refrain. "Better a patient person than a warrior…" (Proverbs 16:32).

Jesus knew well ahead of time what difficult situations He'd be in. And because He is God, He knows what painful conditions we will face. The good news is that He gave us, those who have accepted Him as Lord and Savior, a way to live through difficult situations. Remain under divine calm.

Remaining under divine calm, you become fruitful during fearful moments. You move and operate in the power of obedient Love to Jesus Christ. You have decided to surrender yourself and the chaotic moment to Christ. "It is in you we live, move, and have our being." Being able to regress reactive emotions is not possible in our flesh. When giving in to the will of the Holy Ghost, one can subdue the instinctual urge to retaliate and then take on a servant's heart. Now that's Jesus. When you see someone having a self-controlled demeanor in an intense moment, you know you see Jesus in action.

Points to Remember about Self-Control

- Surrender to the Holy Spirit and listen quickly to its leading

- Subdue harmful instincts by all means

- Experience divine calm in heated moments

- Regress reactive emotions and learn proactive skills

Draw and journal a time in your life when you have experienced self-control through adversity.

Draw Here

Journal here.

_____

_____

_____

_____

_____

_____

_____

_____

_____

Part 3

Why Mature Fruit Is So Necessary

Living in Abundance and Eternity with Jesus Christ

When problems or conflicts arise, and they will, you can choose to suffer with or without the Love of Jesus Christ. To suffer for Christ leads to a fruitful life here on earth and an eternal reign with Jesus forever in heavenly places. This primer focused on your choice to reign with Christ because it centered on applicable ways to problem-solve by modeling Godly characteristics in times of distress.

Manifestation is an event, action, or object that clearly shows or embodies something, especially a theory or an abstract idea. When the pressures of life squeeze you because you chose to model Jesus, you will experience the Love only Jesus can give and comfort that only His Holy Spirit provides. "I will not leave you comfortless: I will come to you. Yet a little while, and the world seeth me no more; but ye see me: because I live, ye shall live also. At that day ye shall know that I am in my Father, and ye in me, and I in you. He that hath my commandments, and keepeth them, he is that loveth me: and he that loveth me shall be loved of my Father, and I will love him and will manifest myself to him" (John 14:18-21). You need the Love of Jesus to bring forth the fruit of who you are and your God-given gifts despite your trials and tribulations. Bearing fruit from your God-given gifts is when you glorify God the most. You, now displaying his grace and mercy through your obedient Love for Him, yields in you Love made manifest by His Holy Spirit, which is peace, kindness, joy, self-control, gentleness, goodness, patience, faithfulness. The indwelling Christ will shine in the dark and chaotic moments of your life when unbelievers see that in you, they will want to know how to receive God's favor. That is when you share the Love of Jesus Christ and His gospel story.

Circumstances or problems become like that of fertilizer in an orchard field. If a believer suffers abuse, bullying, oppression, terminal illness, depression, trauma, unfamiliar territory, hostile environments, etc., know that when connected to Jesus Christ, you can endure it and still bear much fruit in your life. Gardener Jesus can prune you through these painful and uncomfortable moments. He sees the fruit in you, and he wants to yield it. Let Jesus use your difficulty as fertilizer.

He knows how to take everything and use it for His glory. "All things work together for the good of those who love Christ Jesus and are called according to His purpose" (Romans 8:28).

Jesus does not want you and I to have an abundant, fruitful life just here on earth, either. He wants to dwell with you and have you reign with Him forever. Unfortunately, you cannot reign with Him if you will not suffer with Him. "If we suffer, we shall also reign with him: if we deny him, he also will deny us" (2 Timothy 2:12). That is why Jesus bids us stay connected to the vine. He is the vine, and we are the branches. "I am the vine; you are the branches. He who abides in Me, and I in him, bears much fruit; for without Me, you can do nothing" (John 15:4-6).

What we do here, in Love (Jesus), remember that God is Love, and Jesus is God, and that affects eternity where Jesus dwells. The sun is an energy source for all life here on earth and it is the Son, Jesus Christ, who is a life source for all dwelling and abiding in Him. Fruit bearers will see the Son face to face. "They will see his face, and his name will be on their foreheads. There will be no more night. They will not need the light of a lamp or the light of the sun, for the Lord God will give them light. And they will reign forever and ever" (Revelation 22:4-5).

Aside from just being fruitful here, our goal is to dwell in the house of the Lord. "I did not see a temple in the city, because the Lord God Almighty and the Lamb are its temple" (Revelation 21:22). This place is in Christ alone. Your character is being developed through the tribulation so that you can look like Christ Jesus. That is how God the Father will see us... through the lens of His Son's blood that was shed on the cross at Calvary for sinners—you and me. Upon accepting that we are sinners and confessing that "Jesus is Lord" and believing that Christ died and was buried and rose again on the third day, Jesus ultimately saves us and seals us with His Holy Ghost. Christ is preparing a place for us. This place is in Him. Everything about this garden oasis of a home is symbolically a representation of Himself.

Even a river, which even now is a water source to most farming communities, is a representation of Christ, who is Love. Worth repeating. God is Love. Jesus is God's Son. Jesus is God. Abide in Jesus' Love to bear fruit in your life and dwell with him forever. Now, on earth, as we bear fruit, Jesus is the river of life flowing out of us. We are well-nourished in being connected to the vine. "In this 'forever' place, Jesus is that river in the city of God, the holy place where the Highest dwells" (Psalm 46:4).

Suffering in Christ leads to a fruitful life that nourishes us and others. What you have sown in Christ leads to an abundant harvest now and forever. So be encouraged to endure suffering when choosing to surrender all of who you are and your gifts to Christ Jesus, even in chaotic times. Your reward is abundance in peace, joy, patience, gentleness, goodness, kindness, self-control, and faithfulness. All this is Love. If we love Jesus, we will keep the laws of God that are now written on our hearts. We choose to suffer because we love Jesus, and if we love Him, we obey His commandments even in times of persecution or conflict. Our obedience is our Love for Jesus Christ. He sends us His Holy Spirit to help us follow through difficult times. Compliance is what produces fruit in our lives. We must trust this pruning process. Have some fruititude in your attitude and live abundantly here on earth and reign with Jesus in eternity.

Part 4

Fruititude Recipes with Chef Lucia Olivero to celebrate building or rebuilding broken relationships in Love.

My friend and sister in Christ Jesus, Lucia, and I produced a cooking video together for a recipe that is in my book "Fruititude: Growing Spiritual Fruit through Adversity!" Lucia and I partnered up as to where she shared her original fruit recipes to complement one of the characters from a vignette. One of the characters, named Sherry, witnessed God's love in the moment of a broken family matter. Sherry is a personified cherry fruit. Making "Lots of Love Cherry Pies" is a perfect recipe to help bring love and healing to a family being restored. After experiencing the fruit of the spirit in Fruititude, enjoy making precious healing memories with a restored family of God.

For more information regarding Lucia's recipes go to her website, where recipes can be downloaded or shared: www.GreenOliveCooking.com.

YouTube to see how to make recipes: https://www.youtube.com/c/GreenOliveCookingChannel

She has a playlist titled "Fruit-titude."

Lucia Oliverio Bio

In my family, like many others, food embodies memories and is a vessel to create new ones. I remember vividly while growing up, my Italian immigrant mother and grandmother telling the stories associated with the traditional southern Italian recipes they were teaching me to make. That food-memory connection was passed down, with birthdays smelling of gnocchi and chocolate cake and summers bringing back memories of gardening with my dad. He still carries a knife in his pocket, ready for picking whatever is ripe and ready to eat whether it's fruit or vegetables. We especially love eating tomatoes from the vine and feeling the juice run down our faces.

As an adolescent, I grew up in my parents' Italian restaurant, "La Dolce Vita," although as an angst teen at the time, I was not at all interested in the family business. All that changed when I turned 21. I was diagnosed with an auto-immune disease, Multiple Sclerosis (MS). The diagnosis changed my life. I began to focus on the importance of maintaining a healthy lifestyle and found myself once again back in the kitchen.

My passion for creating healthy food led me to earn a Bachelor's of Science in Nutrition and Food Science. I have been teaching cooking classes at the Sacramento Food Coop since 2008, began La Cucina Italiana catering in 2014 – 2016, and to this day, make regular appearances on KCRA Channel 3, Good Day Sacramento Channel 31, Fox 40 News Channel, ABC 10 Sac & Co., as well as volunteer at various food banks, adult daycare institutions, and recovery communities. I currently live in Northern California with my husband, Bill, on our family farm with chickens, rescuing cats, dogs and any other animal that needs a home.

The Green Olive Cooking Philosophy

The Green Olive philosophy is cooking should be fun and uncomplicated, creating the best memories with your family in the process. Recipes should be simple, taking the freshest ingredients and elevating them.

At Green Olive, our goal is to provide great products that will enable you to make memories with your families. Products that do not purport to do what they claim can lead to frustration, and potentially negative memories. All of my products are tested in my kitchen as well as my family and friends' kitchens to ensure they are innovatively designed and perform to what I consider the highest standard "a home kitchen."

You can find me:

https://www.youtube.com/c/greenolivecookingchannel

Facebook: greenolive cooking
Instagram: GreenOliveCook

https://GreenOliveCooking.com

Search "GreenOlive"

NOTES

NOTES

Lots of Love Cherry Pies

Lots of Love Cherry Pies

Yield: 1 -2 dozen, depending on size of cookie cutter

3-3/4 cups all-purpose flour
3/4 teaspoon salt
1 cup cold butter, cubed
3/4 cup shortening
9 to 10 Tablespoons cold water

Cherry Filling:
1/3 cup sugar
1/4 cup water
2 Tablespoons cornstarch
1 Tablespoon lemon juice
3 cups fresh or frozen pitted dark sweet cherries, thawed, halved
1/8 teaspoon almond extract
egg wash (1 egg yolk and 1 teaspoon water)
coarse sugar

Preheat oven to 400°F.

Lots of Love Cherry Pies

1. In a food processor, combine flour, salt, butter, and shortening. Blend until crumbly.
2. Gradually add water and blend until dough comes together in a ball.
3. Remove dough from processor, divide in half, and cover each half in plastic. Refrigerate for 1 hour.
4. In a large saucepan, combine sugar, water, cornstarch, and lemon juice and whisk until smooth.
5. Add cherries and bring to a boil. Cook and stir 1 minute or until liquid thickens.
6. Remove from heat and add almond extract. Set aside to cool.
7. On a lightly floured surface, roll out one half of the dough to 1/8-in. thickness.
8. Using approximately a 4-inch heart-shaped cookie cutter, cut out 12 hearts.
9. Place 6 of the hearts to a parchment-lined baking sheet.
10. Using approximately a 3/4-inch heart-shaped cookie cutter, cut out small hearts in the center of the large heart from the remaining 6 hearts.

11. Spoon about 2 tablespoons of cherry mixture onto the center of each solid heart.
12. Brush edges of the heart pastry with egg wash.
13. Place on top with a cutout heart and press edges with a fork to seal.
14. Brush tops with egg wash and sprinkle with sugar.
15. Bake 15-20 minutes or until crust is golden brown and filling is bubbly.
16. While Cherry Hearts are baking, repeat with remaining dough and filling.
17. Let pies stand 5 minutes before removing to wire racks.
18. Serve warm.

NOTES

_____

_____

_____

_____

_____

_____

_____

_____

_____

_____

_____

NOTES

Joyful Orange and Fennel Country Salad

Joyful Orange and Fennel Country Salad

Serves: 4 – 6

    4 oranges, medium sized
    salt
    olive oil
    ½ fennel
    balsamic vinegar
    mint for garnish

1. Peel 4 oranges and cut into bite-size cubes.
2. Salt the oranges and drizzle generously with olive oil. This will allow the salt to bring out the juices in the oranges.
3. Thinly slice the fennel. Use a mandolin if you have it.
4. Add fennel with the oranges, toss, and season with more salt, if needed.
5. Plate orange fennel salad.
6. Garnish with a drizzle of good-quality "syrup-like" balsamic vinegar, fennel fronds, and mint.

NOTES

_____

_____

_____

_____

_____

_____

Calming Blueberry Smoothie

1 cups blueberries, fresh or frozen

1/2 ripe banana

1/2 cup liquid, dairy, non-dairy or coconut water

1/4 cup walnuts

1/4 cup oats

3 Medjool dates, pitted

1. Put all ingredients in a blender and blend until smooth. If a thinner consistency is desired, add more milk.
2. Pour into a cold glass and enjoy!

NOTES

Shyreece D. Pompey

Slow-Roast Tuscan Grape Pie - "Italian Schiacciata"

Slow-Roast Tuscan Grape Pie - "Italian Schiacciata"

Serves 8-10

1 egg white
1/4 cup sugar
1/4 cup olive oil
1 1/2 cups flour
1 Tablespoon baking powder
1/2- 3/4 cup of white wine or water, enough to make a smooth and workable dough
1 pound grapes*, halved
1/2 cup walnut, chopped
zest of 1 orange
sugar
egg wash (1 egg yolk and 1 teaspoon water)

Slow-Roast Tuscan Grape Pie - "Italian Schiacciata"
Preheat oven to 400°F.

1. Mix the egg, sugar, flour, olive oil, baking powder, and enough wine or water to obtain a relatively soft dough. Knead until it is smooth and roll (about ¼-inch thick) out to make a sheet large enough to line a cookie sheet pan.
2. Grease a cookie sheet pan and line the bottom of it with half the dough.
3. Fill the container with about 3/4 of the drained grapes; gently squeeze some between your hands as you add them. Sprinkle sugar, walnuts, and zest over grapes.
4. Roll out the remaining dough to cover the grapes. Try to get the dough to be about the same shape. Place rolled-out dough on top of grapes and sealing the edges.
5. Brush egg wash on top of "Schiacciata."
6. Spread the rest of the grapes on top of the "Schiacciata." Lightly press them into the dough.
7. Top with a sprinkling of sugar.
8. Bake for about an hour, or until the crust is browned.
9. When it is done, it will be approximately 1 ½" thick; the dough is primarily a container for the grape filling.

*You can vary the recipe. Some cooks use considerably more sugar, and others put chopped walnuts within the Schiacciata and sprinkle them over it. Still, others sprinkle anise seeds or rosemary leaves over the Schiacciata. In contrast, walnuts and rosemary are sometimes used together, anise seeds are used alone.

NOTES

NOTES

Kind Strawberry Oatmeal Squares

Kind Strawberry Oatmeal Squares

Yield: 12 - 16 bars

1 cup old-fashioned rolled oats
3/4 cup all-purpose flour
1/3 cup light brown sugar
1/4 teaspoon kosher salt
8 Tablespoons butter, melted
2 cups small-diced strawberries, 10 ounces
1 teaspoon cornstarch
1 Tablespoon freshly squeezed lemon juice
1 Tablespoon sugar
vanilla glaze, optional
1/2 cup powdered sugar
1 teaspoon vanilla extract
1 Tablespoon milk or any liquid of choice

Preheat oven to 375 degrees.

1. Line an 8x8-inch baking pan with parchment paper so that parchment paper overhangs two sides like handles.
2. In a medium bowl, add oats, flour, brown sugar, and salt. Mix until evenly distributed.
3. Pour in the melted butter into dry ingredients and stir until mixture forms clumps and all ingredients are evenly moistened.
4. Set aside 1/2 cup of the crumble mixture to be used for topping.
5. With remaining moistened ingredients, evenly press in the bottom of the prepared parchment-lined pan.
6. In a bowl, place strawberries, cornstarch, lemon juice and sugar. Mix well to evenly distribute.
7. Place strawberries onto oatmeal layer and evenly spread out.
8. Sprinkle the ½ cup reserved oatmeal crumble mixture on top of strawberries.
9. Bake the bars for 35 to 40 minutes or until the strawberries are bubbly and the crumb topping is golden brown.
10. Place the pan on a wire rack to cool completely.

11. To prepare the vanilla glaze, in a medium bowl, add powdered sugar, vanilla, and milk and whisk until smooth. Add more or less liquid if you prefer a thinner or thicker glaze.
12. Once bars have completely cooled, evenly drizzle the desired amount vanilla glaze over strawberry oatmeal squares.
13. Lifting the strawberry oatmeal squares out of the pan, using the parchment-paper handles, place on a cutting board, cut into squares and serve.

NOTES

_____

_____

_____

_____

_____

_____

_____

_____

_____

_____

_____

_____

_____

NOTES

Apple Goodness Breakfast Protein Shake

8 ounces milk, dairy or non-dairy

1/2 apple, chopped

1/2 cup ice

3 Medjool dates, seedless

1 Tablespoon ground flax seed

1 Tablespoon almond butter

1 teaspoon ground cinnamon

1 teaspoon vanilla extract

1. In a blender, add all ingredients and blend until smooth. If a thinner consistency is desired, add more milk.
2. Pour into a cold glass and enjoy!

NOTES

Faithfully Sweet Peach Tiramisu

Faithfully Sweet Peach Tiramisu

Makes 4 individual dessert martini glasses

½ cup mascarpone cheese

½ cup homemade ricotta cheese

1 teaspoon vanilla

4 Tablespoons sugar, divided 3 and 1 Tablespoons

½ cup whipping cream

2 cups peach nectar or ½ cup peach liqueur with 1 ½ cup peach nectar or juice

1 package of ladyfinger biscuits

2 large peaches, pits removed and cut into thin slices

mint leaves, for garnish

4 martini glasses or other glass dishes suitable for serving the individual desserts

Making the Mascarpone Cream:

1. In a large mixing bowl, combine mascarpone and ricotta cheese, 3 Tablespoons sugar and vanilla. Stir until well combined and smooth. Set aside.
2. In another large mixing bowl, add whipping cream and 1 Tablespoon sugar until it forms stiff peaks.
3. Add whipped cream to mascarpone/ricotta cheese and gently fold in until combined—do not over-mix.

Assembling Peach Tiramisu:

1. In a shallow bowl, add peach liqueur and dip ladyfingers in just enough to moisten them. Ladyfingers can be broken as necessary to fit martini glasses as you build peach tiramisu.
2. Spoon a small amount of mascarpone cream into the bottom of each martini glass.
3. Add a layer of ladyfingers.
4. Add a layer of peach slices.
5. Repeat this process with another layer of each, ending with sliced peaches on top. Reserve a little bit of ricotta/mascarpone filling and 4 peach slices.
6. Refrigerate and let rest for at least 2 to 3 hours. This will give biscuits time to soften and absorb peach flavors.
7. Garnish with a dollop of cream, peach slices and mint leaves (optional).

NOTES

NOTES

Gentle Pear Crostata

Gentle Pear Crostata

Serves 6 – 8

1 premade pie crust
4 cups pears, diced or sliced
2 – 4 Tablespoons sugar, depending on pear sweetness
1 teaspoon flour
1 lemon, juice
1 teaspoon vanilla extract
1/4 teaspoon cinnamon
pinch of salt
egg wash (1 egg yolk and 1 teaspoon water)
sugar to garnish

Preheat oven 350 degrees.

1. Place all ingredients in a bowl, toss and taste for sweetness.
2. Place a sheet of parchment paper, size of pie crust, on work surface.
3. Lightly dust parchment paper with flour and place premade pie dough on parchment paper.
4. Evenly spread pear filling out evenly in the middle of the pie dough, leaving about a 3- 4-inch border.
5. Fold outer edges of dough up and over fruit, pleating as needed until all the dough is gathered.
6. Gently brush the pie crust with egg wash and lightly sprinkle with sugar.
7. Bake for 40 – 50 minutes or until the crust is golden brown.
8. When Pear Crostata comes out of the oven, if there are juices running out of the crostata, use a pastry brush to gather juices and brush juice over pears. This will give a nice-finishing look to the pie and the pears won't look dry. If there is so excess juice, you can also choose any type of jam, add a few drops of water, and brush onto fruit.
9. Cool before serving.

NOTES

NOTES

Watermelon Salad Vinaigrette

Watermelon Salad Vinaigrette

2 cups watermelon, cubed

juice of 1 lemon

2 Tablespoons balsamic vinegar

1 teaspoon honey

6 Tablespoons olive oil

1 Tablespoon Dijon mustard

salt and pepper

1. Puree watermelon cubes in a food processor until they reach a uniform texture.
2. Add the remaining vinaigrette ingredients and mix well.
3. Serve over green salad or fruit salad mix.

NOTES

_____

_____

_____

_____

_____

_____

_____

_____

Frutitude Plush Toy Characters

Collect all nine Fruititude Plush Characters. Remind someone you love that they too can overcome many kinds of adversity and live an abundant life.

Visit
http://www.queenofovercome.com/fruititude-growing-spiritually.html
Begin your collection of all nine Fruititude Plush Characters as they become available.

Sherry's Love
Orangie's Joy
Blupaul's Peace
Grapella's Patience
Strawrene's Kindess
Applina's Goodness
Peaches' Faithfulness
Pairence's Gentleness
Waterton's Self-Control

ABOUT THE AUTHOR

 Shyreece D. Pompey, retired Public School Teacher in 2015, is now a faith-based Author. *HOPE: It Will Not End with My Death* is another book that challenges the heart to endure times of suffering with grace. Shyreece received her master's degree in Educational Leadership shortly after being diagnosed with a rare Stage IV lung cancer. Despite the illness, Shyreece diligently served on nonprofit boards and held offices that positively impact local communities. Being trained as a Stephen Minister equipped her to face her on-going medical challenges while helping others with traumatic situations. Overcoming insurmountable odds to become a professional teacher for 17 years was Shyreece's childhood dream.

Shyreece Pompey, born and raised in the Michigan / Indiana area, now lives in Woodland, California. Shyreece is married to Minister Douglas W. Pompey of 30 years and is actively involved with her three grandchildren. Nothing brings Shyreece greater joy than watching Jesus work in the lives of Believers living in a fruitful relationship with Him. Growing in the image of Jesus Christ is the reward now and dwelling with Him forever is the ultimate gain.

RESOURCES

The Holy Bible. Keystone Giant Print Bible (King James). The National Publishing Company, 1997.

Bible Gateway. www.biblegateway.com.

Biggs, Matthew, et al. Vegetables, herbs & fruit: An Illustrated Encyclopedia. Buffalo, Firefly Books, 2006.

Schlessinger, Laura. Bad Childhood Good Life: How to Blossom and Thrive in Spite of an Unhappy Childhood. New York, HarperCollins Publishers, 2006.

Strand, Robert. Nine Fruits of the Spirit - A Complete Devotion Series – Love, Joy, Peace, Patience, Kindness, Goodness, Faithfulness, Gentleness, and Self-Control (New Style), 1999.

ACKNOWLEDGMENTS

I could not have finished this book without the developmental editing of spiritual friends in Christ Jesus, **Larry and Beverly Brown**. I also want to thank **Dr. Norma Loomis,** a professional Christian Counselor, who is a dear friend and gave me the courage I need to write every day even in the most difficult circumstances of my medical journey. The personified fruit characters would not have come to fruition without the talented artists **Kelsey Jakeway** and **Belinda Wieszczyk**. I am extremely grateful for the talented professional Chef **Lucia Olivero** and how she skillfully and prayerfully created delicious fruit recipes for families to make as they build or rebuild their lives with meaning and sacrificial love.